CW01081298

Boys' Night Out in the Afternoon

Tim Wells lives in Stoke Newington, London, where he edits *Rising* magazine. He enjoys Chinese food, reggae music and fondly remembers the water margins of Liang Shan Po.

Also by Tim Wells

A Man Can Be a Drunk Sometimes but a Drunk Can't Be a Man
If You Can Read This, You're Too Close

Boys' Night Out in the Afternoon
Tim Wells

Donut Press

Published by Donut Press in 2005.

Donut Press, PO Box 45093,
London, N4 1UZ.
www.donutpress.co.uk

Printed and bound by G&B Printers,
Unit 4, Mount Road Industrial Estate,
Mount Road, Feltham, Middlesex,
TW13 6AR.

Donut Press gratefully acknowledges
the support of Andrew Mitchell
Consulting, Arts Council England,
Business Link for London,
Collage Arts and Prevista.

ISBN: 0954198379

for General Echo

Acknowledgements are due to the editors of the following publications in which some of these poems first appeared: *Artefiction* (Stride, 2000), *Breakfast All Day*, *Chiron Review*, *The Daily Planet*, *Gargoyle #41*, *The Illustrated Ape*, *Oral* (Sceptre, 1999), *www.thepoem.co.uk*, *www.shu.ac.uk/proof*, *Reactions⁵* (Pen & Inc, 2005), *The Slab*, *Still*, *www.thundersandwich.com*, *The Trump*, *Wake Me Up Before You Fargo* (Plains English, 2004), *Yeast* and *YoMiNoMo*.

Contents

Boys' Night Out in the Afternoon

When the Water Rises, So Does the Boat

It took him some time
But he managed
To sleep with a string of girls
Whose birthmarks
Made up
All the punctuation
Of modern English grammar.

The full stop was easy enough.
The exclamation mark came too quickly.
He took one girl out to dinner
And then back
To his split level flat
Just because
The two moles on her cheek
Resembled a colon.
The semi-colon,
A Japanese design student,
Was harder.
The question mark,
Obviously,
Was hardest of all.

Next,
He thinks he'll try
Girls whose freckles
Make up words in Morse code.

Space

So
in the Second World War
my grandfather served in submarines
He said
that they stank
The men sweated all the time
and sweat
and condensation
dripped from everything –
from the bunks
from the metal
from the light bulbs
from the very men themselves
The air was rank and heavy
hanging dense
like the oil that smeared everything
Mostly men just lay in their bunks
There were two men to a bunk
one awake
at his post
the other sleeping –
a constant turnaround
so that the beds never got cold
and the lice never went hungry
Above my grandfather's bunk
he stuck a picture –
it was a picture of himself
standing alone

arms outstretched
head back
blowing a kiss at the sky
He looked tiny
He was in a field
alone
with mountains behind him
and the blue, blue sky
spread out like an ocean
My grandfather would lie back
and put himself
between those distant horizons
where he once stood
The other men
had pictures of wives, girlfriends, lovers, pin-ups
But my grandmother
sent this particular photograph
to my grandfather
and it was this
he told me
that made him realise
what a rare woman she was

Born to Drink P.B.R.

Chugging 'em down.
C-list motherfucker on Avenue A.
Dressed like a Viet Nam vet'
going to a bowling alley
on a third date:
"You weren't there, man!"
Keep that music crying into my beer
'cos I've done tonked my honk.
'What Made Milwaukee Famous
(Has Made a Loser Out of Me)'.
Sure, I know that song,
and plenty others besides.
Yeah, you can skynyrd to my lynyrd,
but get a brew first.
P.B.R. Sounds like a military 'plane.
A seaplane with two floats,
a fat Grumman engine,
and a rear-facing gunner.
Ladies – please do your soliciting discreetly.
Even the stuffed deer heads
wear redneck caps.
One has a big day-glo orange
sports stadium wavy finger
stuck over his antler.
But look at it this way,
his glass eyes get to look at us
making animals of ourselves
every single day,

and that's got to be entertaining.
The shpiel might be smut
but it's the only bar
where a gentleman can always be found.
Two bucks for a beer,
one for the girl in the hat,
and twenty-five cents for the jukebox
to quarter our loneliness.
My country loving ass,
grained with the dirt of the city,
ground with the crank of the gears grating
in my late shift head.
Bosses got me running
in the hamsterwheel
of work ethic and shit jobs.
The more I make, the more I owe.
"Buffalo wings?"
Well, the waitresses pass their time
gambling on who orders what.
There's a killer in the kitchen in 70s clothes.
On this chicken frying night
I'll be happy just to get a beer
as cold as the King's grave.
Happy just to shut the place
and make it home
without falling flat on my face.

I know, I was that soldier.

Paint It, Karen Black

Saturday morning, it's my habit,
coming back from the shebeen,
to get beigels;
chopped herring for there and then
and cheese for the morning
I've yet to start sleeping for.

In the early hours, there's a beautiful
but cross-eyed girl serving the bread.
It seems they only ever let her
work the night shifts.
I'm never sure if, when she smiles,
she's tipping me the wink.

Daily, advertising thrusts
its bump and grind into my face:
you pays your money,
we makes your choice.
With her,
it's the uncertainty I love.

Another Long Story

In the movie
the break up is over
with less violence,
the drug scenes
more glamorous;
a little sister written in,
wringing hands and pleading,
"Don't … oh, don't."
During the airport taxi ride,
the soundtrack slips
into a song I hate
but the actor loves.
The in-flight screening
elicits a tear
at the lovers' climactic kiss.
The stewardess
pours me coffee,
pats my shoulder
and says,
"Tired, hon'?"
Once home,
rhymes will be internalised,
I will contain emotion
with words;
I will not write this poem.

On Being Expelled from Eton for Shagging Tallulah Bankhead

I never went to Eton,
Nor shagged any Hollywood sirens.
But if I'd had the background
And the privileges that money provides,
Then I'd have been there, mate.
Been there, pink gin in one hand, dick in the other.
The 1920s were made for a bloke like me.
Brilliantine, lady air pioneers, bobbed hair, and Mack Sennett.
The decade that roared.
I've read nearly all of Fitzgerald, even *The Vegetable*.
I'd have fitted right in.
Me, Timothy George Wells, Esquire.
A lost generation, groping its way in the dark.
Oh, Tallulah,
A girl who, reputedly, bedded forty per cent of British aristocracy.
British, not English.
That's a lot of nobs.
We're talking proper bad girls here.
Bad girls with a sense of class.
Alabama girls thrown out of daddy's house for "immoral proclivities."
Girls discovering sex, drink, parties, and fabulous frocks.
Ah, that I was a feckless aristocrat
With an absurd moniker
And an even more ridiculous nickname,
Motoring to the Hotel de Paris on a sunny summer morn
With the star of *Thirty a Week*.
She throws the car round a bend,

One hand on the wheel, t'other on my thigh,

Eyes on my Petronious.

I nervously quip a saucy epigram from Martial.

She nuzzles my ear and whispers,

"I've been called many things, but never an intellectual."

Oh my dear, does it require an academic to teach the facts of life?

The First Lord of the Admiralty, William Bridgeman no less,

MI5, the Home Office,

All concerned for our morals.

But us lads at Eton are dining out on our salad days.

This scandal, like me, will be sat on.

Seduced by the girl as pure as the driven slush.

She's always skating on thin ice

And everyone wants to be there when it breaks.

My grandfather watched her films.

He died coughing black lung in the 1990s.

Tallulah's last words ...

"Codeine! Bourbon!"

My only regret is the playboy life

I never had ...

On being expelled from Eton for shagging Tallulah Bankhead.

Well, it's better than Spanish flu, coal mining, the General Strike,

And what my family really did through the 1920s.

Snake in the Eagle's Shadow

Boys are intrigued
with whatever can kill;
plague, buckin' broncos
and fighter planes fascinate;
bear pits and tiger cages
suck them in
with quicksand efficiency.
Boys quickly learn
the meaning of venomous;
noses pressed against
vivarium after vivarium,
vipers described as such
in vivid red type.
Boys are not interested
in constrictors
(except for the big ones).
Girls also like snakes,
but for different reasons.

The Big Dumb Ox

Hemingway considered Wyndham Lewis an arse; he described his eyes as "those of an unsuccessful rapist". On hearing that Lewis was to be introduced to James Joyce in Italy, Hemingway asked him to pass on a pair of shoes to Mr. Joyce.

During café drinks, prior to Lewis' departure, Hemingway put into his keeping a pair of shoes carefully wrapped in brown paper and tied with string. I'm sure there's no need to tell you how cumbersome a pair of shoes are, anywhere other than on the feet; especially the shoes of a person with as big a pair of feet as Hemingway, and especially on a long train ride through a Europe that prized uniforms over efficiency. Lewis dutifully, though none to happily, carried the shoes on his journey from Paris to Italy.

Upon his first meeting with Mr. Joyce, Lewis produced the package and stated that he had brought Joyce a pair of Hemingway's shoes. Joyce carefully unwrapped the package and lifted out Hemingway's huge, worn brogues. He looked down at his own diminutive feet and forever after thought Lewis an arse.

One must remember that this was Paris in the 1920s – the Paris of Pound, Fitzgerald and Cummings. There was no television and the pop charts were yet to be invented.

I Take the Supermodels Bowling

Sometimes,
after a hard day's cat-walking
up and down
and all around,
pulling faces and poses
and streaking through changes,
sometimes
the supermodels phone me up.

"Oh Mr. Tim …"
they say,
"… please take us bowling."

So,
I meet them.
I meet them
at the beigel shop.
The beigel shop
at Finsbury Park.
The one where
the girl who appeared naked
in *The Sunday Sport*,
the one where she works.
They don't eat
but 'The Gap Girl'
likes to watch.
And then we bowl.

Naomi,
leading up,
has a decent shuffle
but is prone
to falling flat,
giving all the Chinese kids
who pack the alley
a good look at her arse.
"It's all in the follow through,"
she says.

Kate Moss
is a good sniper
but has problems.
She pictures the pins
as shapely women
and clearly channels
a lot of aggression that way.
However,
being waiflike
she has to use
an extremely light ball
and thus dissipates
much of the energy
she exerts.
Her insistence
on fashionable clothes
is also a hindrance.

I enjoy bowling
but the 'überbabes'
don't come out too much.
Obviously,
bowling
at Finsbury Park
is a very limited
photo opportunity.

Ben Sherman

In the 70s, people thought the future
would be flyless suits and hoverpacks.
I knew it would be no change really,
drunken yobs in Ben Shermans
kicking the shit out of each other.
Feels good to have backed a winner.

The Fish Must Not Be Allowed to Leave the Deep

We can betray ourselves
By our own intelligence

During the war
The Soviets were
Intelligent enough
To train dogs
To associate tanks
With food

Meat was placed
Beneath parked tanks
And with landmines
Strapped to their backs
The dogs became
Fast, low, hard to hit
Canine bombs –
The idea being
That the life
Of many an Ivan
Would be saved
From the fearsome firepower
Of the Teutonic tide

The dogs were
Intelligent enough
To remember
That the meat
Was previously to be found
Beneath Soviet tanks
And once sent into action
Promptly ran under
The advancing T-34s
Ignoring the Nazi panzers
And forcing
An entire Soviet division
To retreat

Stalin duly
Had the dogs purged
As traitors to Mother Russia

Trials of Life

In bars,
Wildlife shows
Always intrigue.
Those that
Feature apes
Often raise a ruckus.
Those belching,
Farting,
Hairy beasts.
That fine society
Which functions
On who
Scratches who
And who
Picks whose fleas
From who.
Whose round is it?

Heaven's Just a Sin Away

In a perfect world
on my way home from the pub
I would see:
a fight
a vomiting teenager
a stand up pair of shoes in the street
a blow job taking place
and a crying girl.
Of late
there's been a dearth of weeping women.
I live in Stoke Newington
which is far from perfect.
Even for one as easily pleased as I.

My Own Private Ida Lupino

Not even the completeness of rain,
just the languid 'I might or I might not'
indecisiveness of dull, dreary drizzle.
I'm already reconciled to not leaving the house.
There's a Sherlock Holmes film on the telly;
it's not going well for him. Moriarty,
"the very genius of evil",
is about to snatch the crown jewels.

Indeed, Holmes is in a tight spot
but he'll pull through. I'll make do with hot Vimto.
Outside, all I can see is the sky pressing down
and my underpants flapping on the line.
I should go bring them in
but they're only underpants:
clean of me, moist with London.
There they hang – my flag of surrender.

The Sun Also Rises

Hemingway enjoyed the six-day cycle races in Paris. Several times he started to pencil out a short story about cycling but he finally concluded that the drama of the reality was too chain-to-pedal to capture on paper.

Few of Hemingway's friends shared his enthusiasm for the races. This often irked him. On many occasions, he extolled the virtues of the focused cyclists who'd compete against their own limitations as much as they struggled against the other cyclists. A rider had little to help him but a tube connected to a hot-water bottle filled with cherry brandy which was lodged beneath his shirt.

In April 1926, Hemingway was accosted by a drunken American tourist who decried his love of the races, calling it "guff". Hemingway pointed out the mental and physical discipline of the cyclists but the tourist quickly poo-pooed this; he then continued to denigrate the European athletes. Hemingway grew angry. Finally a challenge was made and a wager agreed wherein the tourist and Hemingway would cycle the Champs Elysées, the winner pocketing fifty francs.

Hemingway, a big man and then in his prime, was ill at ease on the bicycle procured for him. It belonged to a much shorter man. He promptly picked it up and carried it on his shoulder, a glass of beer in his free hand as he trotted the course. His long strides and relative sobriety easily enabled him to beat the cycling, though breathless and giddy, drunkard.

At the Arc de Triomphe, the agreed finishing line, Hemingway awaited the red-faced and puffing loser. The tourist threw down his bicycle and loudly proclaimed Hemingway a cheat. Unable to stomach an insult this time directed at himself, Hemingway promptly knocked the man down with a stiff right-handed punch. He snatched the collected fifty franc purse from the stakeholder and threw the money at the prostrate loudmouth. As the notes fluttered down, Hemingway spun on his heel and, calling out "For your doctor's bill", retired to the nearest café.

All the Sad Young Men Without Women in Love

Poor Scott,
Careering atop the roof of a 1920 taxicab
Along deserted Fifth Avenue
On a hot, purple, Sunday night.
Bawling, for having everything he wanted
And knowing he'll never be so happy again.
Poor Scott,
Swimming at St. Raphael,
Buzzed by the French naval aviator
In love with his wife.
Scott holds a towel and dries himself.
Afraid for her to pass out in the company they kept:
His crazy, jealous wife.
Poor Scott,
Just the name makes me sad.
The novels, the stories,
The crack up,
The ridiculous questions,
Dust on the wings of my bookshelves.
Poor Scott,
It was never that small.
Hypochondriac in all but writing.
If only your juice was as stiff as ink.
Whiskey isn't everything,
Soda isn't anything.
Poor Scott,
Gone into that cheap Irish love of defeat,

Betrayal of himself.
A failure as a success
And a failure as a failure.
Even his love for those closest to him
Was an attempt to love.
Poor Scott,
Hemingway's alcoholic
Without the capacity.
Talking with the authority of failure,
Across the same table,
Hem, the authority of success.
Ring was bigger than the diamond,
Hem larger than himself.
Poor Scott,
Studying the books on the Great War,
Collecting photos of the battlefields.
A missed test of manhood:
Uniformed but never left the United States.
Hemingway shows off the scars.
Scott haunted by how he'd behave in battle,
At Hem's shoulder, not crossing the road in traffic.
Dead, December 21st 1940.
In that year all of Fitzgerald's books
Sold a total of seventy-two copies.
Hemingway's shotgun added the punctuation.

Madison Time

Three of us had driven up from Los Angeles. Roddy and myself were to read. We didn't know it was an old folks' spread 'til we got there.

They weren't ready for the Poetry Group, and the organiser was somewhat surprised at our relative youth. It seemed that, up until then, he'd had no competition for the affections of the ladies. I can't speak for Roddy, but I'd no intention of giving him any.

Roddy did his Wing Biddlebaum bit and smoked. I'd been looking forward to a drink at the bar, but there wasn't one, so I killed time looking at the notice board instead. The plugs were mainly dead women's belongings and burial plots. I'd have settled for a whiskey mac.

I heard music from down the corridor, and so far it had been the only sign of life being lived, so I went to see what was happening.

Looking into a room I saw a gaggle of fifty-something-year-old Koreans circling in time, mostly, to music spun by an old Disquette-type record player. There were two couples and a dozen single women who had to dance alone. Their empty arms held onto to partners they'd craved, lost, or never had.

There they were, shuffling around the room, alone, as the Korean boss lady barked:

"1 2 3 4, 1 2 3 4."

They were preparing for an America that had died with JFK. Only no one had told them.

I put my face to the glass of the door and waved. Most just looked at their feet as they 1 2 3 4ed around the room. One lone women, though, she looked back, smiled and then waved too.

I felt better; if no one could Howard Keel through the song in their heart, here at least was a soul whistling the refrain.

Next door the poets were solving the problems of the world. None of them was dancing.

Overlord

"... and yeah," she says,
"when I was younger I worked in McDonald's."
I stir my coffee and ask about her name badge.
"It had three stars."
I tell her Patton had four.
Her eyes eagle to meet mine.
"He had more responsibilities ...
but I could command hamburgers
on the Normandy landing beaches
... if I wanted to."

Oysters and Snails
(with thanks to Agathias)

Let Christina Ricci herself,
let Thora Birch and Claire Danes
and all the company of Love
curse me, shrivel my shank
with their hate,
if ever I turn to the love of boys.
O goddesses,
from sliding errors and slipperiness guard me!
To sin with girls is sin enough:
Simon Callow may have the rest.

Songs That Are Whistled

Here's to the lonely country girls
in shotgun city apartments,
miles from home
with only phone calls
and breakfasts and songs
served to hipster losers
to convince themselves
they made the right decision;
to the herb gardens
on kitchen tables;
to pine air fresheners,
scrubbed vegetables,
birdsong,
and fire engines
that shrill outside;
the potted plants
grown with love
in fired china.

I Don't Know But I've Been Told ...

The Eskimo have seventeen words for snow.
The gene pool of the Arctic Circle
Is not as broad as the tundra is vast.
Buggery is a common form of birth control.
During lovemaking,
Some Eskimo
Tie blubber to a string
Which their inamorata swallows.
As the gentleman completes himself
He tugs the string,
Causing her to gag
And firmly clench
The muscles of her fundament.
Apparently,
Dried caribou meat
Is better than blubber
Due to its leathery texture.
The engineering is not important.
Obviously,
In an igloo
There's only so much to do.
Beneath the aurora borealis,
Recreation and leisure facilities
Are few and far between.
With little occupation,
One's imagination and behaviour
Will travel to some strange places.

With the arrival of contraception
And central heating,
Much has changed for the Eskimo.

L.A. Rain

you can see the neon and never see the light
the footsteps of all those who can afford not to walk
readily washed away
men's feet in women's shoes

the footsteps of all those who can afford not to walk
water dancing hipshots across the oiled smear
men's feet in women's shoes
the hookers of Santa Monica Boulevard

water dancing hipshots across the oiled smear
water finds its own level
the hookers of Santa Monica Boulevard
the gutters full to bursting

water finds its own level
only cream and bastards float
the gutters full to bursting
fresh water gives life, this beats down

only cream and bastards float
waitresses course through the channels of Chinatown
fresh water gives life, this beats down
dirtiest rain I ever saw

waitresses course through the channels of Chinatown
readily washed away
dirtiest rain I ever saw
you can see the neon and never see the light

Up in Michigan

During the Depression, Hemingway visited Henry Ford's Rouge Plant in Dearborn, Michigan. As with many moguls, the industrious Ford was not only concerned with constructing excellent automobiles but also worried by the plight of humanity. With this in mind, his Ford Motor Company periodical, *The Dearborn Independent,* published from May 22nd 1920 on, anti-Semitic diatribes, later published complete as *The International Jew.*

Ford was an early exponent of motivational management. At the time of Hemingway's factory tour, a 'boosting sign' was tacked to the wall adjacent to the production line. "REMEMBER WHAT HAPPENED TO THE DINOSAURS", it read. On spotting it, Hemingway made his way over and considered it at length. As his group paused, Hemingway took out a pencil from behind his ear. Beneath the picture of a waddling diplodocus he added: "The dinosaurs were self-employed tradesmen."

Minding the Gap

On the job two weeks.
Doin' a training course.
Less than two hours in this room –
Already bored.

Opposite,
There's a big pile of girl –
A generous girl,
A girl in a short skirt.
A skirt way too short
For a room
Where the air-conditioning
Doesn't work.
And hey!
It's spring.
My mind's wandering.
Ridin' that train.
And my eyes …
Keep drawing down
To her thighs.

In the 'getting to know you' bit
We started with,
She revealed
She was in the Naval Reserve.
Now I can't but look
At her navy knickers.

Mmm,
Navy blue knickers.
Navy blue knickers
and Wren's cap.
See, I just can't
Keep my mind
On what's at hand.
It's not even
that I want to look.
It's just that I can
And I can't stop …

Mmm,
Marbled flesh.
Well, to be honest,
More that someone's
Taken a blue biro
And repeatedly traced
The Victoria Line
Up and down
Her inner thigh –
All "mind the gap"
And the heady
Finsbury Parkness
Of my finest moments.

She's squeezing out
Lemon juice looks.
I don't blame her,
I can't stop myself.
The people here
Must think I'm a right perv'.
New job and all,
Not the impression
I wanted to give …
Though accurate.

Office Politics

'Look at him.' She seethes.
'See how he drinks his tea:
with the spoon still in the cup!
You know what that means?
He's too lazy to take it out,
too worried about leaving a little stain on his desk,
or just not sensual enough to lick it.
Either way, he's a cunt.'

I dunk my biscuit
and wonder if this makes me a wanker.

My Bitch Up

Burning Geronimo through the East End,
the motor skittish at jump, stop, start.
Music blasting out the windows, slapping
Joe Public in the face as we roar by,
tossing the used notes behind us;
dirty knees and carpet burn noses.
Each staccato burst spent, surly, and spittin'
in the eye of all the pocket money massives.
On Commercial Road, some
City boy lone ranger races us red light
to red light, every green a pistol shot.
At Limehouse, John John faces him
and mouths, "Ours is stolen."
The silence: single mum heavy.
Someone drops the sprog.

Why I'm Called Oblique

I don't know why they do
But strange things happen to me
Maybe it's because I'm strange?
But I don't think I am
(Particularly)

For instance
The bands I prefer
All start with the letter B –
Buffalo Springfield
Bo Diddley
The Band
The Beach Boys
And best of all
The Byrds

Now
I'm well aware
This is no more
Than an alphabetic
Coincidence of taste
I'm not some kind of lunatic
Whose musical likes and dislikes
Are determined by the letter B

But when girls
Come round to my house
And skip through my records
That's exactly what they think

Silver Dagger

She took a blade
and carefully shaped the powder
'til,
in five looping lines,
it spelt her name;
each letter
three inches high,
hopeless white,
and sure of itself.

Across town,
I was writing my name in the snow;
my handiwork
neither as neat,
nor as measured.

In Praise of Hiroo Onoda

In the jungles of romantic endeavours
I am a lost command Japanese sniper
Still fighting the Second World War
Philippines, 1974
Focused
Disciplined
Making an excellent job of it
But wrong
Wrong
Wrong

Fiesta

Pamplona. Outside the cafés the wineskins were being passed and the fool was king for a day.

Working its way through the jubilant crowd was a shaggy, mangy bear; a jackanape ruff bobbing around its neck. It made its way slowly, the crowd was tight, and pulling it back by a chain fixed around its neck was a sweaty man, shirted in the flounces and ruffles of dishonesty. The man's free hand clasped an iron bar with which he would thwack the bear to make him dance. The bear would shuffle, *thwack*, weave, *thwack*, and then raise its scuffed paws, only to have its massive shoulder thwacked by the gurning troubadour. A gambolling girl accompanied the pair, shaking and beating on a tambourine.

As they moved past the knots of people, the tambourine would be passed so the crowd could drop coins and monies into it. These were then tipped into a pocket before the tambourine started its infernal rattling anew and the iron bar was again raised to coax new steps from the tired bear.

Lounging in his café chair, Hemingway caught sight of the bear and immediately jumped upright. Although a large man, the bear was bigger. Hemingway downed his wine and reached into the tambourine as it ran in front of him.

The minstrel stepped up at once, shocked at seeing his monies disappear. He started to yell some glottal curse only to be sent reeling backward by the writer's large paw thwacking him in the face.

Hemingway knew all too well that festival, dance and music, these things are all of the heart, of joy, and of life. Though misery is as much a part of life, there is enough without being shackled to it.

The money was tossed to the crowd, which revelled all the more.

Cary Grant's 'Cool for Cats'

(with thanks to Claire De Jong)

"A-mew-sing",
the papers categorised it.
Small pictures
of bunnies and birdies
and meeces
in balsa wood frames,
all hung a foot
from the ground
with saucers of milk
beneath them.
The opening was a blast:
kittens gambolled,
wool was unravelled,
even Will Self smiled.
Cary looked as though
he'd got the cream
and Archie Leach stated
that he'd never seen
so much pussy in one place.
Everything was hunky-dory
'til Katherine Hepburn,
ever one to be
the centre of attention,
turned up with her leopard.
The spotted beast
could be nought
but a catalyst
to catastrophe.

Fur flew and drinks
were spilt.
Amidst a caterwaul
of catcalls
it was left to
a cat-suited Marilyn
to sort out
the monkey business,
which with great aplomb,
she did.
The dapper gent said
he found it
"cathartic".
Oh, Cary Grant …
so suave but
no innocent.

Two Hearts

This foxy, nuyorican,
Salty margarita in a dress,
Wid at tit ude,
Is talking *la vida broka*.
Her beauty could stop a crime.
I'm just selling whiskey
To the Indians.
Rather down those bottles
Than talk *the struggle*.
Trying to show her I care
By getting her drunk.
Heard me read my writing,
Finds my accent *intriguing*.
I'm thinking 'bout
Some porn mag Pocahontas
Lifting her tits to be spunked on.
But she isn't.
She's just a girl and her pomes
And both of us
With a fistful of nothing.

Let the Good Times Roll

When Suzie gets back from drying out,
I'll let her pour the coffee,
talk or keep schtum,
whichever way the milk spills.
Her face won't be a mess,
her clothes will be clean,
her head will be clear.
There'll be a party
and some fool will drag out
all those old punk rock records,
all those ones she loves so much.
There'll be beer,
there'll be juice.
Time will be tight,
tongues will be loose.
There'll be a party,
we'll all be delighted.
When Suzie gets back from drying out,
Suzie won't be invited.

Cinnamon Girl

My Japanese friend
has learned some bad English from me.
She says that this
is what she came here to learn.
Often,
when meaning "thanks" or "goodbye"
I say "cheers".
She uses this same expression as a toast,
only she always mispronounces it as "tears".
I've never corrected her
as besides from being endearing
there is more truth to this
than she knows.

With Rommel in the Desert

As a lad I built models;
Had a damn fine Africa Korps:
Mk. IVs, Kublewagons, 88s,
And, for that Kasserine Pass
Push against Fredenhall, Tigers.
Now older and writing poetry,
I'm collecting middle-class girls;
Initially, to be fair, by default,
But now it's something of a hobby.
The price is higher
And my friends are not as impressed.

Hardly Hardy Kruger

These days
I rarely wake the street up
poppin' my cork.
But it's better
to be the Wehrmacht
dispatch rider,
coasting through
Paris, 1941,
with panniers
full of champagne,
knockwurst,
and frilly knickers –
a powerful beast,
easing my way there,
more the victor
for taking my time.
Better that
than to be
the pizza delivery boy
burning through
Church Street
full throttle,
two-stroke
straining.

And Too Many Byrds Records

Love seeps from me
It steams in my piss
It flakes in my snot
It stinks in my sweat
Love is so much
A part of me
That I could no more
Shit it out
Than I could stop
My heart from beating
Love is my sustenance
My breakfast
Lunch and dinner
It is my water
Beer and spirit
I breathe its breath
Wear its apparel
Walk within its furrow
And live in its abundance
I feel love's colour
On my face
This is no drug talking
This is me
Who put his shoulder
To the world
This is me
Trying hard to be better

Out of Season

In 1941, prior to the Japanese attack on Pearl, Hemingway was in China; ostensibly to report on the war the Kuomintang and Communist Chinese were waging against the Japanese and between themselves, but also to gather intelligence for the American government. His wife, Martha Gellhorn, was also there reporting for *Colliers*.

Hemingway terrified the Chinese by his sheer size. *The Chungking Central Daily News* of April 15th 1941 noted that "Colossal and muscular, he is apparently taller than Dr. Kung, the Vice Premier." Despite this, Hemingway quickly made friends by picking up the local lingo.

The glamorous Mrs. Hemingway could stand neither the filth nor the poverty of the teeming Chinese. Her hands quickly picked up 'China Rot', a nasty fungal infection, and she had to smear her hands with a 'malodorous unguent' and wear gloves. In the rank heat of Shaokwan, this was almost unbearable. Hemingway blamed the infection on her insistence on washing.

Both Hemingways quickly developed a severe case of 'the trots'. Ever the linguist, Hemingway utilised his newfound vocabulary to procure toilet paper from the locals. Unable to communicate, Gellhorn was reduced to tearing up copies of *Colliers* and wiping her arse with her own stories. This rankled her no end.

A Picture From Life's Other Side

I don't live in west London
Where how cool you are
Is determined
By how stupid your name is
Where hip hop climbs like a weed
And bad slang
Spreads like the flu
Not having a problem
Is the problem
Complexes masquerade as complexity
And neuroses
Hunt in packs

I don't live
Where lunch on the move
Is a way of life
Where *jazz*
Is the tears of an un-sated addict
Choose life!
But will life
Choose you?
All you need is love
And the Portobello Road
Seduces itself

The keys rusting
Atop the bus stop roof
Lyricise your search
For something to search for
And the chick in the shades
May look cool
But she's still nursing
Two lovely black eyes
Where the Underground
Is overground
And you can't get enough
Of too much

I do not abide
Where the attention span
Is as long
As the last white line
Where Jamiroquai
Working on a building of love
Is really nailing down the roof
On his musical career

No, I don't live in west London
But I write poetry
And that's bad enough

Sound Man Burial

They carried him box in like a bass bin.
Man, it had the dreadest thud of all.
We was all there, dressed for some
killer diller party night, just one more time.
When they done laying him down,
we supped the bottle an' passed the draw.
Funny how it was youngsters there
an' us here so, like it were east London
an' south inna dance from time;
each group cupping spliff,
trying not to get caught by the other –
these sons truly sprung from these fathers!
By the time the bottles were emptying,
the dance floor was raisin' up;
ska tunes from when we were rude,
rude once more. Prince Buster,
Lloyd Nibbs, Tommy McCook …
the horns blew a welcome
'cos me hear that even in heaven
they have a sound,
but them can't get no Red Stripe beer
fe sell inna dance at night.

Reversing the Polarity

It's a mistake to talk
to girls in Star Trek outfits,
but this one is dressed
as Lieutenant Uhura.

Foolishly, I reply
'Tiberius'
when she asks
if anyone knows
what the T
in James T. Kirk
stands for.
From that, she's keen
to explore our 'connection'.

Her explanation of how
the doors work
on the Starship Enterprise
is not my idea
of 'inthekitchenatparties'
conversation.
When I say
I'm not bothered
if there really is
alien life,
she is not best pleased.

'Look at the odds.
When you consider
the sheer number of stars,
it's arrogance to assume
that we are alone!'
She prods her finger
into my chest to emphasise
the arrogance
on the 'we are alone.'

I sip my beer.
When you consider
the billions of people
on the face of the earth,
doesn't it strike you as telling,
the sheer number of single,
lonely, desperate nerds?

Space ... the final frontier.

Chuck

Nearly perfect in that pissed,
Wednesday night,
After hours kind of way.
Blonde, drunk,
Tight shirt, two pints,
And stood up.
That she was talking
To the likes of me
Raised my concern.
But then, monkeys
Can reach orbit
Without the slightest
Comprehension
Of the technicalities,
Physics or engineering
Of rocket science.
I may be just a chimp
In a NASA suit,
But one day …
Apes will be our masters.

When a Man's In Love It's a Splendid Thing

On the job he keeps it screwed tight,
in a vault, key thrown away.
He knows how many tracks the CD has to run,
where the horn solo will kick in,
where his unpaid bills are,
what page the book,
tossed to the floor beside his bed,
lies open on.
He knows the whole topography of the room
and his place within it;
where tits and arse
and love and passion,
where they course through it.
Having grown up in a block
hearing neighbours,
friends and parents hard at it,
this grunting smacks of the mundane.
He tries to secret the glimmer,
wrap it in silence so that what is his,
remains his alone.
For her, it's the abandon,
the lady rampage, the hair out of place:
all the fistfuls of mayhem she can get.
He's not sure if her "Yes! Yes! Yes!"
is from her pleasure or for his benefit.
He wishes she'd be quiet
and so works that little bit harder,
spurring her on

to that one affirmation more.
He likes westerns,
the badmen galloping into town, guns blazing.
She loves the shadowy allure of the silent greats.

The Torrents of Spring

Hemingway came from a musical family. His mother was a songwriter and opera singer with pretension toward her own music salon. It is not widely known that Hemingway made recordings himself. Scribners thought it a good idea to tie in Hemingway's popular Nick Adams stories – stories that captured the tough beauty of the American landscape and the lives that unfolded thereon – with the emerging country music market. Many of the country songs had a narrative structure and it was hoped that some of the people spending dollars on Lefty Frizzel records might also be lured into purchasing Hemingway books.

In 1955, shortly before helping with the film script of *The Old Man and the Sea,* Hemingway recorded an Arditi song he'd learned in Milan. Benny Martin accompanied him on mandolin. At the time, Martin was with Flatt and Scruggs popular bluegrass band; he can be heard on their hit record 'Dim Lights, Thick Smoke (And Loud, Loud Music)'. However, Hemingway's wife, Mary, thought the song, though rousing, would not be commercial due to its being sung in Italian, and it was never released. A version of Hemingway singing Dock Boggs' 1927 masterpiece 'Sugar Baby' was recorded at the same session and this was pressed. Amazingly, Hemingway plucked out the tune on banjo, a style distinctive of Dock Boggs.

> "Oh I've got no sugar baby now;
> It's all I can do for to see peace with you,
> And I can't get along this-a-way,
> Can't get along this-a-way.
>
> Done all I can do. I've said all I can say;
> I will send you to your mamma next payday,
> Send you to your mamma next payday.

Got not use for the red rockin' chair,
I've got no honey baby now,
Got no sugar baby now ..."

On hearing that his glamorous ex-wife, Martha Gellhorn, considered the song to be about her and that she had remarked that Hemingway sounded "... like a lovesick bloodhound", he instructed his brother, Leicester, to purchase all the available records. These were used for skeet shooting at his finca. Very few copies remain.

Call Me Ishmael

The measure of a man
Is not tattoos or scars.
It is not a string of broken hearts
Neither is it his own.
It is not the cut of the clothes he wears
Or the texture of his hands.
It is not what others say concerning him
Or even what he says about himself.
It is not what knowledge he has learnt
Or even such literature as he can quote.
It is not his integrity
Nor his detachment.

No, it is none of these.
The measure of a man
Is what he does when no one is looking.

The author would like to raise a glass to:

The Sweeney, the Tighten Up crew (Mistah Brown, Tim P and Champion),
Francesca Beard, Phil Silvers, Tim Turnbull, Meg Lee Chin, Mao Ying,
Mr Sherlock Holmes, Eek A Mouse, Sarah Kobrinsky, Max Barabander, August
Kleinzahler, Prof Richard Holmes, Liang Shan Po, Martial, Ivan Penaluna,
Salena Saliva, Clare Pollard, Tenor Saw, Roddy Lumsden, Doug and Dinsdale,
the George Robey public house, Cheryl B, Junjo Lawes, Jenny Wren, Laura
Comerford, James Bell, Asta, Ingrid Pitt, King Tubby, Doc Holliday's, Mo Yeu-
Ing, George S Patton, Nick Adams, Ring Lardner, Adebisi, Charles Middleton,
Shelly Thunder, Hiroo Onoda, Trevor Cleaver, Sarah Wishart, John Stammers,
girls with price tags on the soles of their shoes, Niall O'Sullivan, Clarkey,
General Urko, Cody Jarrett, F.T. Marinetti, the horse that Nietzsche kissed,
Drunken Master, Cesar Romero, unruly breasts, Robinson Jeffers, John Citizen,
Ogami Itto, saucy postcards from seaside towns, Sam Peckinpah, Polly, Beowulf,
Bob Wells, Toshiro Mifune, Sven Hassel, Johnny Alucard, Anna May Wong,
Lola Choo, I Roy, Joel Loya, Erwin Rommel, Lo Lieh, the Zanti Misfits,
Ring Lardner, the Mighty Two, Sir Percy Blakeney, Richard Brautigan, F. Scott,
gits and twats, Max Miller, the rocking of the 5000, fops and dandies, Barrington
Levy, crying girls, Amelia Earhart, Sid James, Lord Wastrel, Gert Frobe, Hugo
Williams, Karen Black, Angela Chase, Nathan Penlington, John Poetry, Paul
Lyalls, the Swedish Bikini Team, Sei Shonagon, Yen Li, Cary Grant, star-crossed
lovers, truck bunnies, UK Bubblers, the mice on the mouse organ, downed
airmen, shipwrecked sailors and monkeys shot into space.

Also Available from Donut Press

Stranded in Sub-Atomica, by Tim Turnbull. £10 (plus £1 P&P)

What was that?, by Tim Turnbull. £5 (plus £1 P&P)

Buffalo Bills, by John Stammers. £5 (plus £1 P&P)

The Switch, by Jonathan Asser. £4 (plus £1 P&P)

Cheques, POs and IMOs payable to Donut Press.
Donut Press, PO Box 45093, London, N4 1UZ.

www.donutpress.co.uk